Teaching My Daughter to Mulch

Teaching My Daughter to Mulch

Gardening Meditations

Donna Schaper

Ash Grove Press, Inc.

Teaching My Daughter to Mulch: Gardening Meditations by Donna Schaper

Grateful acknowledgment is made for permission to reprint previously published material:

"Teaching My Daughter To Mulch" excerpted from the book, *STRIPPING DOWN: The Art of Spiritual Restoration* by Donna Schaper. Copyright © 1991 by LuraMedia. Reprinted by permission of LuraMedia, Inc., San Diego, CA.

For information contact Ash Grove Press, 19 Elm St., South Deerfield, MA 01373.

A percentage of every sale is contributed to groups and organizations which work toward creating a safe and healthy world.

Library of Congress Cataloging-in-Publication Data

Schaper, Donna.
Teaching My Daughter To Mulch: Gardening Meditations.

ISBN: 1-886172-19-6
1. Gardening. 2. Spirituality.

Library of Congress Card Number: 94-12045

Printed in the United States of America
Cover Design by Patricia Ouellette
Illustrations by Keelin Sabel

Ash Grove Press, Inc.

Dedication

To Katie Emma Goldstein
that she may also use star dust on hard jobs.

Table Of Contents

Teaching My Daughter To Mulch

I have said it before. I plant too much. Each year I add annuals to spots where perennials grow. On top of hollyhock and baby's breath, I drop zinnias or beans. The competition for nourishment begins.

No doubt my daughter feels the same way as my overplanted garden in the competition for nourishment. Her father and I take care not only of her, but her brothers, and the planet, and our jobs, and our politics. Her father and I also do windows.

Even before our species was born, the earth was too much with us. We should never have reproduced ourselves. There is very little about our biological life that respects either evolution or what we do with our lives. We eat wrong, drive wrong, and most of our backs feel as if we shouldn't even be standing up on such a regular basis.

Our lives are too much for the soil in which they are meant to grow. We are pale green plants, requiring extraordinary amounts of chemical fertilizers. We are biologically immoral, environmentally untenable. I can't imagine why I bother to worry about zinnias or beans or hollyhocks.

1

But worry I do. I don't want my annuals to crowd my perennials, so I have opened new gardens almost every year. I have a little less than one acre on the eastern tip of Long Island. The back of my property descends into swamp, that connects to river, that connects to bay, that connects to ocean. I *own* only the swamp. All those connections take about seven miles to complete.

My first garden was in the front yard, the second in the back. The third will be in back of the back. Pretty soon I will hit swamp, and my genetic repentance and soil-building projects will meet their match.

I began with sand. Tan Long Island sand. That first year, in the front, I added about thirty one-hundred-pound feed bags of cow manure. The second year we mulched the flimsy soil with grass clippings hauled from the yard of almost every neighbor in a two-square-mile district. I panicked only once: What if some of these neighbors were using chemical weed control? What if I was poisoning my own soil with their clippings? It is the same panic I knew from the apple juice scare: What if, in the name of nourishing my children, I had fed them poisoned apple juice? I kept trying to tone down the words poison and panic. It never worked.

No doubt I did borrow some pollution. But at least I didn't pay for it. I hauled it. I even reused the plastic bags in which my neighbors had packed the makings of my new garden. A semiannual dose of lime also helped. This year I have some magnificent rotting hay. The mulch will be better than normal, breaking down more slowly into a more complex nourishment. It might be as good as my compost, or the fish carcasses that now rot slowly below the tomato plants.

I also took my neighbors' leaves. Each autumn we hauled about two hundred bags of leaves, first to the front, then after another century, to the back. The decomposition of the lime and the manure and the leaves and the grass clippings gave us space to plant more than we could possibly maintain. Am I proud of all this hard work and the back that made it possible? You bet. When I'm not humiliated, that is. The whole process is such a perfect example of the repentance of which I am capable: two steps backward, one forward, in that great march toward oblivion that my species is making.

First, I recover *useless* soil by improving it. I march back to a sustainable time. Then, instead of being satisfied with a little, I march forward to a lot. I overextend and overplant in complete imitation of my species' general habit. This one step forward requires more mulch to keep the maintenance low. So far, so good. Neither gods nor genes have rejected my liturgical march back to the swamp.

Mulch makes my confession. I can't possibly weed all three plots once they are in and growing. Also, I need the annual improvement of the decaying mulch. Furthermore, watering this leaky, sandy stuff would cost me and the larger environment too much. In the name of all these sensibilities, I have to get mulch down pretty quickly after the garden is planted. Not too soon, of course, since the soil has to warm. The end of May is usually ideal for the mulching.

This year we shook hands with the ideal time before it eluded us. That near miss is the origin of this long defense of the size of my garden. The idea that I could be happy with two yellow marigolds and a zinnia in a box or a bucket of geraniums and a row of beans is insulting. I don't like the ordinary garden, and I don't like small gardens. God has tapped my shoulder. Maybe the garden is not really overextended. I just know the tyranny of growth so well that I begin to fear it everywhere. What I don't know is how many more gardens I'll need to build on this shy acre to be happy. I begin to wonder if I can leave anything alone.

Comfortable white Americans like me plant gardens that are too big. With us, it's a way of life. God forbid I should be satisfied with a normal eight-hour life. I work too long at my job, and I work too hard at my garden. I have other excesses, but there is no point going into them right now.

Anyway, my back didn't go out until after I had shaken hands with the ideal. I saw its face, I knew what it would mean to befriend it. We were in the third year of this particular project. It happened in almost the same casual way that the earth could self-destruct. The spring had been extraordinarily wet. I had two gardens to get in and the third needed a good weeding. We had come to the end of May and, behold, the sun came out on a Saturday. I was going to get the gardens in and the mulch down unless it killed me.

Which, of course, it did. I dug and dug and kneeled and kneeled and then dug some more and kneeled some more. All of a sudden I felt a feeling I had never experienced before. My back wouldn't get straight. I couldn't figure out if it was the earth that said no or my body that said no, but definitely the great refusal to carry on had begun. Of course I paid no attention to the warning. I kept digging and kneeling and getting up and down to dig and kneel some more. I dared the garden to kill me.

Which it did.

The dare-to-kill attitude is probably the same attitude that got us into worrying about whose flag to put on the moon. Surely the dinosaurs, as brain got disproportionate to brawn, would have driven cars with the same going-to-get-there-if-it-kills-me attitude that the late twentieth century values so highly. Going fast is part of overextending. If we don't go fast, we don't really have time to do so much. If we don't do so much, then we resign our citizenship in the upper crust. Part of being the upper crust is to go fast enough to use more than our share. The speed and the direction are a lethal combination.

On the same day that my back went out, I had intended to teach my daughter to mulch. She would be my salvation because with her labor added to my labor, theoretically we could *get more done.*

My daughter mulches completely differently than I. I, in the interest of my citizenship, carry as much as I possibly can and carry it as swiftly as I possibly can to its destination. She, in the service of some five-year-old muse, picks up small hands of grass clippings and, like a fairy princess dusting with stardust, places a few of the clippings gently on the head of a Montauk Daisy. She then walks the five-hundred feet back to the clipping pile, picks up another handful of grass clippings and, muttering magical incantations, dusts a day lily or pea pod. She says she is going to start on the raspberries tomorrow, a project that should take her several hundred years.

I want to retrieve soil from swamp and sand ASAP. I don't know how much longer we'll live here; I don't have time to waste; and I don't think I'll be happy with just three gardens. I have too many projects, too many plans. Like the nation of my birth, I have a mission in this garden. My mission is to improve it. I am a veritable machine out there.

A few days post-back and post-chiropractic, I told Katie about my plans to teach her fast gardening. She objected on several counts to the curriculum. She didn't want to hurt her back like I had hurt mine. Therefore she had no intention of overdoing it. She didn't want to rush because rushing got in the way of skipping. She refused the lesson in efficient mulching on the grounds of avoiding pain and having fun. Then she got distracted and skipped away, empty-handed. In the twinkle of an eye, I was alone again in the back garden, mulching away by myself. Katie was deep in the swamp, lifting stones and looking for mealybugs. She was singing some song I couldn't quite hear. Usually these days it's Peter Pan's rendition of "I don't want to grow up."

How exactly am I supposed to teach this child to mulch or, better yet, to grow up? I wish I could conclude that her ways are better, but I can't. Children are not the solution to the problems adults have made. Fairydust would never have tamed the prairies. No matter how much of an environmental romantic I have become, I'm pretty sure somebody had to figure out how to grow enough grain to feed all the people that we have overplanted.

If there is a culprit, it is my childlike ignorance of limits. I don't know how to stop. It's almost as if I need somebody to stop me. Wait till I tell Katie that it's dark and it's time for her to go to bed. She won't want to hear a word of it, and it won't be because she is an American, but rather that she is a child. I'll have to carry her kicking and screaming all the way from the rear garden into the house.

Mulch will be the trick I'll teach her because I don't really quite believe in nature. I think we can improve on nature, that we can make it come alive with living things. Sand grows no spinach. More troubling is the matter of how much spinach we need.

The trick will be teaching my little Peter Pan how to improve the soil without breaking her back, my back, or the earth's back. The farmer in me can't let her think that she can live on the soil effortlessly. The environmentalist in me can't let her think that all soil needs her improvement. My job is to teach Katie what I don't yet know. Yet another repentance, isn't it, to raise our children better than we were raised ourselves?

To spoil soil as a way to improving it? To go just one step forward and one back to a better future? Or, in the telling of these stories, to march forward to a better past?

Plotting The Garden

hinking about what the garden will be is more fun than the garden's being. The plot is the all season pleasure; the execution the short season's work. Early winter while the ground is still warm through its long summer basking, and before the first snow flies, right before the turkey is cooked, is one of the great times for the gypsy gardener. The one who loves to move things.

Almost everything will tolerate a move this time of year. My mums love long division in this season as do the day lilies. They wonder how their colors will mix for a long time before they actually do so.

When writer E.B. White (author of *Charlotte's Web* and many other works) wrote about his wife, Katharine S. White, the author of the famous *Onward and Upward in the Garden*, he remembered her as every autumn placing bulbs in the ground, "calmly plotting the resurrection." (1979) He wrote these words in the introduction to the eleventh issue of her famous gardening book:

"As the years went by and age overtook her, there was something comical yet touching in her bedraggled appearance on this awesome occasion—the small, hunched-over figure, her studied absorption in the implausible notion that there would be yet another spring, oblivious to the ending of her own days which she knew perfectly well was near at hand, sitting there with her detailed chart under those dark skies in the dying October, calmly plotting the resurrection." (1979)

White was more than right about the nature of pleasure. It is something we steal from the darker days for the lighter days. Autumn gardeners are wrong to only focus on the bulbs. There is more to do than just plant. Evaluation and wandering about are also very good November tasks. See who is there. What happened.

I liken this task to that of the women at the grave in the New Testament who confuse Jesus with the gardener. Now you see the flower of your faith; now you don't. Even the big resurrections are off season in a parabolic way: they happen much too quickly. Then, before and after, even for years to come, we harvest their meanings. Just as we plan in the fall for happenings in the spring, we remember in the winters of our days, the messages of the previous springs. At dusk we hear again the sounds of birdsong.

One November I was madly searching for something to do in the garden. I like to do a little piece of its labor every day and to think about what I might do with my few brief moments all day long. It is the same plotting, dragged out, enjoyed, strategized, then done. On this day, I said, "I will move the worms." They lived deep in the compost. The compost was hot. I knew of some leaf piles where I had already buried fish heads. By the way, if you have not plotted tomatoes in the early winter by planting fish heads in places predestined, do so. It works. The tomatoes love the calcium (or something) about the fish. This early winter day I knew I could still dig the ground. I loved the idea of the worms pulling up their down blanket of snow and snuggling in. So I dug cruelly into the compost and halved a few dozen worms in my clumsy forklift. I put the worms under the leaves, with the fish heads, and dug them in. I actually heard one thank me. They never liked that neighborhood in the first place. The dead were left to bury the dead.

The next spring I had an astonishing number of worms, both in that year's tomato patch and in the old compost. I thought of calling in the Zero Population Growth people to confess my sin. Reproduction in the worm world was clearly out of control.

Another good plot for the winter gardener is to clear brambles. They don't hurt so much when you have on more clothes. As W.S. Merwin puts it in *The Lost Upland* (1993), "the hard brown knots of ancient blackberry kingdoms" love to move. But only if the ground is very friable. They can't penetrate ice crystals.

Hen and chicks in the rock garden will also move around well at this time of year but be sure to cover them with lots of leaves. Keep the leaves off the iris which will probably have poked through the fall soil if it has been too warm. Be judicious with the leaf blanket though; iris disease loves leaf mold.

Many of us fear, of course, that the garden is more mental plot than actual plot. Someone mean actually said that "what a person thinks of a garden is entirely projection." I forgot his name on purpose. The problem is precisely the opposite. Projecting the garden, mentally, spiritually, emotionally, is gardening. We drag out its meanings through all our parts, through all our seasons. We extend the season this way. Plotting is more like solar tunnels than anything else. It is something we put over the actual ground to let its processes go on longer than they naturally are able to manage.

Gardening, as a whole, is the tension between our projections and our plots. In autumn, we notice what really happened last year. I have to admit that I also moved worms too late one year, and they all died. That death was not a projection.

In the interior garden of the autumnal season, we deal with the reality of what we have seen and the potential failures of our projections. Then, in tension with our hoped-for plot, we plan another garden anyway. Anthony Trollope tells of going down to London on the train with what he thought was a good handwritten manuscript of a long novel. The publisher said, no, thank you. On the train going home, Trollope laid his bulky bundle down on his lap face down and began writing a new book on the back pages of the rejected one. Some of our gardens get rejected by the great publisher as well. We turn them over and begin the story again.

If the beans got disease in the north corner, we should not put them there again. But we can try some other crop in the place where they failed. Plotting is comprehending failure and rising from it, to fail again or maybe even to live.

The great gardener and writer, Vita Sackville West came to the conclusion that you can't come to a conclusion. Whether to hope in the autumn for a better garden in the spring—or to wait for plotting till the advertisers make their January colonization of the tables next to our chairs—is a serious question. The autumnal plotter will make more conservative choices; the armchair gardener will spend money on behalf of less realistic fantasies.

I cannot explain why some gardens are spectacular and others mediocre and still others spectacular in certain plots and mediocre in others. These displays can change annually also, as we all know. I failed to grow the Italian basil three years in a row. This year they all came up so beautifully that some actually took frost. I couldn't use them all. Christopher Fry, in Part Two of *The Lady's Not For Burning*, says "I gave you mystery and paradox and what you want is cause and effect." (1994) How right he is. Our autumnal walks in the garden are not searches for causes or effects; we are there to visit the mystery and paradox of what lived well and what failed to live well. We are visiting the death bed of a friend. It is no time to talk about how she smoked too much.

There are those whose grief in the fall is so large that they swear they will not plant another garden. I've heard them say, "too much work, too little reward." Their plot is grass growing where dirt now stands. They have become afraid of the dark. The part of myself that identifies with the biblical sower whose seed fell on bad ground is also afraid of the dark. Here speaks the child in every gardener, the one who has not been around long enough to know about gardens and gardening and the way unearned failure this year is just last year's unearned version of success. But who is more foolish, the child afraid of the dark or the man afraid of the light? The light will come back in the spring. We will need to have seed in our hand. Our business as gardeners is to outwit the inevitable. The inevitable includes that season that came to

Katharine White, as sure it will come to you and me. The best we can hope for is that we get a few things in the ground for someone else's spring. Imagine the grief of those who love and surround us to lose us in the fall and then our color in the spring!

It's not like there are a lot of other choices. People say they don't want to *return to nature* as if there was someplace else! We only have these choices, to plant or not to plant, to grow or not to grow. Gardeners who move to nursing homes have the same choices. They just have to live in the spiritual space that autumn provides all year long. They have to move to the mental memory of the garden and find someone to cultivate that memory.

Here I am not talking about hoeing but about conversation. Maybe the nursing home move, which terrifies everyone who has ever thought of it, needs its own plotting. Perhaps here is the real reason to keep those little garden journals which I hate so much. They feel so removed from experience. But if one of our moves is to a wheelchair, or we fear it might be, perhaps a journal can be the hoe to our memory which we'll need in the (gulp) autumn of our years.

These moves all need the same plotting as our plot. We don't need reminders of the courage that is needed for gypsy gardening. So many of us use gardening as a hedge against the necessity of moving and changing. We plant a garden so we can look settled. Feel settled. Imagine ourselves as settled down.

The garden I hoe was planted and developed by a couple that lived and worked in New York and summered in Amherst, Mass. It is a superb garden. They only enjoyed it part of the years.

Then, three years after they retired here, after, no doubt, desiring that retirement for decades, she died. He managed another three years alone and is now in a nursing home in Maine. I sent him pictures last year of the herb garden.

Freedom, someone wise said, is what you do with what has been done to you. Brownie, from whom we bought the house, didn't get all that he wanted from his garden. Neither did the one all the neighbors call Mrs. Brown. I am writing in her room right now, overlooking her garden: she is not. Amelia Earhart said courage is the price life exacts for granting peace. I need courage to plot the time when someone else will be sitting in what is now *our* place. So did Mrs. Brown. Autumn gardening, the walk through, the stop, look and listen at the bedside of the season's dying offering, is the plot for courage.

Once we get this business about necessary moves into our coffin or our cubby in the nursing home, we can begin to fly again. We have the instinct of the rose. I think of our fall behavior as that of the climbing rose. We have to grab on to something and grow towards the light. The real roses do it in the spring; we have to do it in the fall.

There is no reason not to grow a few real things in the fall. The entire process is not spiritualized. Turnips and carrots do very well here, under leaves, till early spring. I have three solar tunnels that make fresh spinach a possibility on the Thanksgiving table. At thirty bucks each, they are the best garden investment I have ever made. I have Russian Kale that never seems to want to freeze. And the hardy mums last longer every year. But color is what I want. Just a little more to challenge the grey skies of November.

I know I won't get this color but year in and year out, I search for it. Midge Keeble in her book, *Tottering In My Garden* (1989) tells us that "gardening is not the main theme of life. It weaves in and out . . . providing a counterpoint to family, home and friends, giving colour and balance to life, challenges unending, and often a dash of the comic."

We can only want what we can't have. We can't always have it. That I want more from the fall garden than I can get is basic. I am working on that theme and counterpoint in my fall desires. Early winter, late fall, whatever we call the time that the garden dies, is a great time of the year for embellishing the stage on which the rest of life rests. This *rest* of life needs the spiritual and the physical part of gardening to make it well and interesting. As I see it, we have plenty of time in eternity for the resurrection; now we need time to plot.

Teaching My Daughter To Mulch

Teaching My Daughter To Mulch

Three Women And The Theology Of The Gypsy

he garden has always been a seriously spiritual place. As such it has needed a theology, a picture of its God. Many too simple have been offered. I think of the agrarian mythology, "a simple peaceful farming people" as George Washington liked to call us. Or I think of the suburban theology: two marigolds and a zinnia. Simple. Easy Maintenance. Looks exactly like our neighbors. Or I think of nearly any fundamentalism which promises simplicity in exchange for interpreting your own reality.

Good garden theology is based in garden reality. Garden reality is tension, not harmony. Moses coveted grapes. Jesus went to the garden to weep. The garden of Eden is our origin. People go to the garden *alone* while the dew is still on the meadows. There they pray and meditate; they walk and talk with God.

I think of Vita Sackville West and May Sarton and Katharine White as my gardening theologians. Reading any of them is almost as good as a visit to a holy place. They manage the tension of the garden by showing us what is there that is holy and what is missing in the holy. Each of these women advises the gypsy in us.

What is the gypsy? She is the restless part in us, the part that moves.

Gypsies tell us what they have learned by going the road themselves. They show us how full the garden is as spiritual source—and then they point to its frustrations. By doing both, they adhere us to our gardens and point us ever beyond them.

Gardening is a full enough experience to show us our own limitations. It is a light thrown on what is full in us and what is partial in us. Gardening announces what we can do and can't do. I can't grow sweet peas. Yet. I can't miss on greens. So far.

While each of my three gardening friends found enormous satisfaction in the garden, each also found disturbance. They mistrusted their love of the garden, knew that it was *just* a refuge from the more important and difficult world. As gypsies, they were suspicious of contentment.

The theology of the gypsy is here: part is whole. Limitation is normal. Suspicion is an aspect of trust. But never be satisfied with just part, go for the whole. Never get limited by suspicion; trust even suspicion. Keep moving toward something you know you're not going to achieve. Gardening is a great laboratory for that kind of spiritual process; it substitutes something temporal and small and specific for something eternal and large and grand.

Many women use the garden theologically in these ways. We find and enjoy imperfection there. We try to improve on it but fortunately aren't able to. A similar partial journey through imperfection was the journey of these three famous women as well. They longed for refuge and then mistrusted it. They too remembered their failures in the garden long after they had forgotten their successes. They glimpsed eternity from a patch of tulips.

Many women use Vita Sackville West, Katharine Anne White, and May Sarton as their spiritual mentors in the garden. We try to get spiritual and gardening guidance from them. A mentor is a supervisor who risks becoming a friend; each of these women does that, albeit in an almost icy way.

Mention the name of May Sarton and many women will say that she fully revealed the prize of solitude in the garden. Mention the name of Katharine White and many women will say that she taught them the art of thinking about the garden. If Katharine was all mind over matter, then our third mentor, Vita Sackville West was all matter over mind. Mention the name of Vita, and many women will say that she supervised their sexuality while making it look, for all practical purposes, as though she were talking about gardening.

Gardens resurrect the spirit, the mind, and the body. That is their complete spirituality. Each of these women supervises one of those connections; Sarton, spirit, White, mind, Sackville West, body. Not that Sarton doesn't understand sex, or Vita spirit, or Katharine a bit of all three, but rather that each has a particular window on the ways that dirt resurrects. Each has a spiritual specialty.

May Sarton can actually drive a person quite crazy with her urgency about solitude. On the one hand, she seems to have more friends and guests than anyone else. On the other, she seems quite unhappy to have them. She frets. If it rains the day after M. comes, then how will she get the tulips in? If she didn't have such successful books, then she would not have so little time in the garden. The garden brings her peace; the friends hassle. So why does she spend so much time with the friends and so little time in the garden? If there is an answer, Sarton will find it. God knows she is on its trail with all the energy she has. Like any gypsy, she keeps moving toward the answer without genuinely expecting to find it.

Likewise Katharine White was an overly productive person. She managed the *New Yorker* with its various writers, two children, a famous husband, and a sparkling literary life. Then as she and the *New Yorker* aged together, and it needed her less as years went by, she began to garden. Her husband describes her mingling manuscripts with seed and bulb, editing one Amos Pettingill of White Flower Farms with the same dark pencil that she used on Thurber. She put on a suit in the morning and came out of the garden looking as officious as when she entered. Whether pruning or penciling, her hands remained busy. Her greatest gardening pleasure was the arrangement of the flowers for lunch. Once an editor, always an editor.

Katharine lusted after the product of the garden, its beauty, the filling up of space with colorful peace. May Sarton and Katharine White both give endless descriptions of window sills cradling blossoms, of pages unwritten unless eyes are graced with flowers.

Why do I feel that entering either home would evoke the same sensibility? Calmed, coiled beauty, enduring no fools, welcoming while critiquing all comers? Are you, the guest would be subtly asked, a taker or a giver, good enough to enjoy these flowers or this mind?

Not one of these women was modest. Their gardens weren't modest, and they weren't modest. Each had a realistic assessment of her own value. They were right not to nice their time away with the hoi polloi. That this absence of modesty indulged some of the worst freedoms of the rich is another matter. Class contains privileges and some use the privilege class brings to expand leisure time. These three rich women used their privilege to grow flowers and, through flowers, to risk the constant resurrection of solitude, thought, and sexuality. The gypsy spirit knows that there are plenty of people being nice and too few risking practical resurrection.

Of course their freedom is an embarrassment to that other kind of woman writer, the one without domestic help or secretary. Katharine's complaint in one of her letters to May tells all: "Household and secretarial help, i.e., the lack of it, is my greatest enemy." (Davis 1987)

The theological linchpin for each woman is that she thought she deserved happiness, leisure, wealth, and fun. I am actually warmed by this expectation. It brings out the better gypsy, the better rover. We so rarely hear women of this stature whine. They complain instead. Poor and middle class women would do well to imitate right here: to be more content with our high expectations for life rather than guilty about them. Such an attitude might not make us better gardeners but it would make us better gypsies. And gypsies find God in the least likely places. God is not so much in the better places or the better expectations—or even in my awkwardly given advice in this paragraph. God is more likely to be found in the places we can't quite see. Yet. God is in the gypsy stretch, urging us to take a step out into something we can't quite discern so that, from there, we can begin to see.

As I think about moving my garden north, I experience the most fear right here. In the stretch. Can I really expect as good a garden in my next spot? Or as good a life? Or is one of the punishments for restlessness decreasing pleasure? That backhanded way in which fear tells you that you'd better stay put, because "a bird in the hand is worth two in the bush."

This kind of fear would not have stopped Katharine White. She would think her way through it. Nor would it have stopped Vita. She simply didn't understand boundaries well enough to respect them. May would have the fear, admit to having the fear, and then conquer it.

I am most fond of sexy Vita. She was neither more modest nor less rich than the other two. Still I imagine a warmer welcome to the stranger from her equally vivid window sills. Vita was always in love. If not with Virginia Woolf, then with her husband or another of her male or female lovers. She had that kind of bilingual lust. Fortunately, for the snooty morality of England, she had a garden too. The garden skimmed off some of the cream. You have the feeling, because of Vita, that gardening is most accessible through the body, not the mind or spirit.

In her garden the colors were bright, the privacy carefully planned, the refuge a top priority. When Vita fell out of love, it was to the three shades of cosmos that she went for comfort. Would she have understood as much of the peace of a garden without the lovers? No, it was the risky love she brought to the garden that animated it. Would either of the more prudent and prudish women understand her risky love? May, yes, because May is a lesbian who has to understand sexuality; Katharine probably not. Never forget that when May's vivid mind went to look for a metaphor to describe who Katharine was to her and other women writers of the period, she chose the metaphor of *Mother Superior*. Katharine was our Mother Superior, she said. Less sexy you can't get.

Vita had more of the gypsy in her, and she probably saw more pictures of God through her body than mind or soul could capture. At Sissinghurst, Vita Sackville West's castle home, her unconventional gardening ideas came into their own. First she practiced a kind of ruthlessness in her gardens. Never keep things that don't work. Don't give them another year or another chance. Hers was an unplanned garden, a spontaneous garden, one in which wild experimentation was always taking place. Her gardening columns for the *London Observer* endured from 1947 to 1961, showing that she had enough new ideas to carry on.

As a result of these several immodesties, we are well mentored. We have some good if not kind friends. We have a few pictures of what the Resurrection looks like to a few good dreamers. To be shown the point of view of the mind opens the garden to evaluation, to reflection, to hard analysis of what best use to put to dirt, of what to let go of and what to keep. These gardens make decisions about the last days and what belongs in them.

One of the ways in which each of these women is a gypsy is her discontent, her roving spirit, the way she was never quite satisfied right where she was. Another is each one's specialization. If it is true, as I think, that Vita was more body than soul or mind, Katharine more mind than body or soul, and May more soul than body or mind, then the missing part is what is longed for in the garden. The discontent is directly related to the shadow rather than to the fulfilled part.

Katharine frets over what to plant and when to plant it. Vita frets over missing color. May frets over missing emotion, over what she calls in her book, *After the Stroke* (1988), time to watch the sun slide across her porch. The garden satisfies the part in each that it can satisfy and dissatisfies the part in each which is underdeveloped. Gypsy theology understands that we are all like this, only parts, only spokes, only able to see what we can see of God and garden and not really very much more.

Many people, and not just gypsies, are specialized to the point of eternal longing for what we don't have. Not quite happy right where we are. We can learn a little about the parts we don't have and even learn to use them, but we have to keep moving *north* or *south* to exercise them.

To be shown the point of view of the spirit is to forgive every garden's product for not being all that it might have been, to make a priority of the process, the gift of all that time alone, whether or not it panned out. The spirit sees in a fuzzy way. Through the fuzz, it sees beauty.

The mind clarifies. It sees very clear lines, demarcated plants, whole systems. The mind really does want to know what the soil test said. What type of nematode did what. It keeps records for succession planting.

To experience the body as it experiences the garden, not just as work but also as lust, is to connect to the earth, to adore it, to understand why recreation and procreation are so firmly partnered in sexual activity. This is why Christians say that we believe in the resurrection of the body, right before we mention life everlasting. To know the garden through the body is to touch it, caress it, not be able to pass by the peonies without giving them a wave.

Nevertheless, enter the gypsy's permanent dissatisfaction: wouldn't it be fun to combine the trinity into a unity, to have that richly erotic experience of the body, mind, and soul all being invited out to play in the same afternoon? Possible only in sex? Only in writing? Only in gardening? Only in heaven? Only in wishful conversation as mentors become friends? The answer is a yes to all the possibilities as long as you don't expect to see every one, every season. And as long as some afternoons, all you see is shadow.

Katharine is summed up by her husband E.B. White as every fall planting bulbs and "calmly plotting the Resurrection." (1979) Exactly! As women gardeners see it, the resurrection of the body and the spirit and the mind all develop from the holy dirt wholly experienced. Or they don't. They finally either do or don't.

The gypsy knows what it means when perfection doesn't quite happen. She may even enjoy the not quite happening parts. It is from within the knowledge that it is not quite perfect that we go into the gypsy theological stretch. From that level of reality—which does take a mind, body, and soul to recognize that something is missing—we begin to see. That seeing is as much God as records well kept, sex well consummated, or light on a front porch well viewed. God may be all three. Gypsies can only be one at a time.

Gypsy theology is most astute in understanding matters of idolatry. Human is part not whole. God is whole not part. But gypsy gardeners aren't humbled by that. They are exalted.

Teaching My Daughter To Mulch

Teaching My Daughter To Mulch

Gardening At Night

he latest thing in gardening is lighting the night. There is actually a night light store near me, and every gardening catalogue I receive has a more elegant display of lamp posts than the last. I have been gardening in the dark for so many years now that I find this trend catching up to me more than I to it.

When you know that you are a gypsy, and not just one in the garden, you know that gardening is something you can do anywhere, any time. I have been known to weed the Marriott parking lot. I have also gone in search of the green at convention centers. I no longer evaluate their landscaping services, but I do make sure I find out what bow they have made to what they call nature amidst their concrete. I travel a lot and often find myself far from my own garden.

When I am at home, I garden at night because I work all day and because I have an absurd discipline requiring me to touch soil daily. I count a day lost in which I don't garden the garden.

By that I mean, on a bad day, touching it and pulling two weeds; on a good day, giving an hour to some worthy plot. This discipline has kept me alive to the soil and allowed what would otherwise be an unmanageable garden to be unmanageable in a more interesting way. The discipline keeps garden in the category of prayer: it is my rug. If I can't get there five times a day, I can bow to it at least once.

Often in the darker seasons of fall and winter, I find myself moving rabbit manure at twilight, or pulling up stakes at midnight, or hoeing while the moon comes up. I make no claim for fertility added or earned by night gardening, but I know that an Aztec or Mayan would. They would garden at night for the advantages; I do it for the conveniences.

In the 1300s the belief was widely circulated that humans are wiser when the moon is waxing, and therefore any work needing thought, such as planning a layout, should be done at that time. Greek and Roman gardeners believed that the moon affected plants because the sap would wax and wane with the changing phases. Now we know that tides and moons are connected, then they only assumed it. More than one person plants by horticultural horoscope, which strikes me as just another way of stating personal convenience.

Surely more majesty was deposited during Creation than we could ever, in our scientific mode, imagine. There was more order, more intention, more interplay in the genetic disposition of things than even prayer and praise can comprehend. When I plant at night, after a long day of other kinds of work, I am connecting my life to these original mysteries. I am insisting that soil touch me, that night and day differentiate me, that the daring of creation be something I remember. I am a pilgrim back to that second day, when darkness took the name of night and light the name of day.

My days are otherwise a conspiracy to make me forget that I am created, ordered, intended, even genetically mysterious. In the day, gardening reminds me of the enormity of creation. But at night, with the stars as my guide, I am creation's participant-observer, kin to the divine, illuminated, re-created.

Certain constellations have compelled the human mind since the beginning of time. We think of Orion or Ursa Major. Some say that science and mathematics had their origin in the questions posed by the night. No doubt religion has its own settling of accounts with the questions of the night. By day I work on these as a recession-beleaguered pastor. At night, in my garden, I co-create when I'm not gazing at the stars. Or being held spell-bound by the moonlight. Or imagining the time when, once again, gardening will be as natural as my day job.

The best job for the night gardener is weeding. There are always weeds. They are everywhere. Pulling a couple gives that sense of satisfaction that the gardener lives for, and also has a sneaky way of keeping that activity known as *weeding* a parttimer in your garden. I would so much rather move the strawberries, or dead-head the petunias as a day's gardening activity, than go *weeding*. Weeding brings us up to the place we should have been; other garden activities take us somewhere. That's why weeding is often so depressing; night is a good time for depressing work. We can't stay long in the night garden. We will get involved in the stars soon enough and find our way back into our covers. Going utilitarian before the stars grab us is always a good idea.

Night gives us more than a quick utility and a long star gaze. It provides more than connection to the ancients who respected both light and dark equally. Night gardening has a kind of poetry. We both see the big weeds—and pull them—and don't see the little ones. The garden actually looks a lot more well kept at night than it does during the day. "If the poet is rich in anything, the poet is rich in points of view." So says Robert Frances in his poem dedicated to the Juniper tree. (1976) Night gardening increases our points of view. It replenishes our stock of garden memories for the next day.

The night view of the garden is not a falsified one. It is not like make-up that a sour face puts on to look better. It is simply a different one. It is not the working face so much as it is the non-working face of the garden. We rarely pick at night. We rarely hoe. We don't spend time improving the garden. It seems fine just the way it is. What we do at night is appreciate it. Some say that even keeps the plants in a better mood and growing better. The Psalmist tells us that in the day is goodness; at night, song. At night the garden sings. In the day it practices the goodness of feeding us and startling us and frustrating us. At night it moves to a deeper rhythm. That rhythm is more important than most of us know. Rather we know its importance but rarely experience its existence. For those who want off the merry-go-round, gardening at night is a real stop of the swirl. We can even pull a few weeds before we get on to the magic.

My favorite garden hymn is really a Christmas hymn. It is "Let All Mortal Flesh Keep Silence." The night garden keeps the silence. It achieves calm. It has learned the trick of quiet. This is what the saints do. They become quiet enough to hear God. There is no doubt that God is calling each one of us. The problem is that there is too much clatter and clutter for us to hear.

The next way to hear God is to prepare ourselves to hear in unlikely places. Every saint can tell you that God came to him or her in an unlikely way. Through the burning bush for Moses, the lost coin for the woman of little talent, and the cross for Jesus Christ. I think of the man they call Granny in San Francisco. You probably saw his story on television. He is the longest living person who has the AIDS virus. He has zero T-Cells. He has lived nine years with full blown AIDS. For his work he ministers to AIDS babies. Every time one of them dies he puts a stuffed animal on his wall. The apartment was covered with 1600 stuffed animals, each representing a child he knew who died of AIDS. When the earthquake happened, he said, they all started to fall down. When the reporter asked him why he kept reminders of the suffering of children all around him, he said that the animals reminded him of God and how "God never failed to be with any one of them." God comes to us in unlikely places, even through suffering.

Becoming quiet enough to hear and see God in unlikely places is both the reason to let our burdens down and the consequence of letting them down. When we let our worries go, God comes. More than a few people love that song, "I come to the garden alone . . . " There should be a night version.

There is an enormous field on the corner of Northville Turn-pike and Route 58 in Riverhead, New York. It is probably the most accessible open space within walking distance of my old house. Something new is happening there every season. The field can brim with St. Johnswort, daisies, dandelions, crabgrass, timothy, clover, pigweed, lamb's quarters, buttercup, mullein, Queen Anne's lace, plantain, and yarrow. Or it can sprout grasses too numerous to name. But each does have a name. Not one of these species was here before the Puritans landed. And now they threaten to take us over.

I have already mentioned the strange appearance of weeds at night. Then they carry even more of their divinity. Weeds are as unlikely a source of divinity as we can mention. And yet, and yet. They have a kind of magic, and they also carry a message. First their magic, then their message. According to Sara B. Stein's *My Weeds* (1988), wild oats growing in a field of alternating furrows of spring and winter barley will mimic the habits of either crop, depending on the row. She also tells of a rice mimic that became so troublesome that researchers planted a purple variety of rice to expose the weeds once and for all. Within a few years, the weed-rice had turned purple too. At night we can't see all these costumes. But we see others. And knowing what these plants are really up to amazes us even more as they turn in the light of the night.

Not to respect weeds is to refuse a message from the divine, the message that nature is unbelievably smart and resilient, that plants mean to survive. That message may not relieve all of our burdens but surely when it comes to the big one about our own survivability, we should take a little comfort in the million miracles of the weeds.

The botanical fact about weeds is that they grow in response to human disturbance. The more humans disturb the environment, the more the weeds adapt and grow. Another botanist, Jack Harlan, in *Crops And Man* says, "If we confine the concept of weeds to species adapted to human disturbance, then man is by definition the first and primary weed under whose influence all the other weeds have evolved." (1992)

Ralph Waldo Emerson saw the same thing. He said that a weed is simply a plant whose virtues we haven't yet discovered. Other people have been less kind about the weed. Paul Dickson says that when weeding, the best way to make sure what you are pulling is a weed and not a valuable plant is to pull on it. If it comes out of the ground easily, it is a valuable plant.

There is a formula here for finding God. At first sight weeds are just weeds; ugly, useless, not our plan at all but a foreign plan. A different plan. God often comes to us in precisely this way. In the unlikely place.

There is an old saying about the garden. That the glory of the garden lies in more than meets the eye. God often lies in the same place, in the place that more than meets the eye. At night, our eyes don't confuse us into thinking that we see the truth. At night we know. What we see is shaded. Looking at the shade is another good route to the truth.

Think with me of one more example of a message from God. Mention health care and most people think of doctors. There is no question that doctors are important and necessary to health care, but healing tends to travel another path, a path that does not have M.D. written all over it. Some say that nurses outnumber doctors three to one. In the average hospital stay of five days, a patient might spend less than an hour with a physician. That patient, however, will spend all day, every day, attended by nurses. The point is more about God than about medicine. The God who wants to lay our burdens down is not administering a pill. Zap! Fixed! Burdens laid down. The God who is calling us is more a caretaker. More a watchman. More like a nurse, I think. One who makes sure that hospitals and life don't scare patients or people to death. At night we watch God in the unexpected place at the unexpected time. Sometimes we are even healed of our day.

Teaching My Daughter To Mulch

Teaching My Daughter To Mulch

In The Name Of The Garden, The Garden, And The Garden, Amen

 y text this summer will be three of the seed catalogues I saved from spring. I will use these texts to preach a little sermon about before and after, spring and summer, now and then. (All sermons have three parts and a little conclusion.)

The Clyde Robin Seed Company sent me its 1990 wild-flower catalogue from Castro Valley, California. (P.O. Box 2366, zip - 94546). The catalogue arrived on one of those late winter days that needed outside intervention. I remember both the rain and the fog and their implication that grey was in charge. The cover of the catalogue gave my resistance movement the little push it needed. I am a member of an international resistance movement against the greys. We need all the help we can get. When reality dampens, fantasy is required.

There on the cover was a marvelous specimen of a Califor-nia woman, kneeling, knee deep in yellow poppies and blue flax. She had the look of health all over her face: the white hair that peeped out from under her hat exuded vitamins, her tailored outfit announced that she was in this for fun. (Farm workers are different from gardeners in at least this way: they don't get dressed up to pick.) Behind the sloping field of yellow in conversation with blue, was a trellis that led, Zen-like, down another slope to the cottage. Implied in the photo was the idea that this grand lady lived in this humble cottage. At her breakfast table were melon and whole grains; in an ancient pitcher made for poppies and flax, flowers graced her meal. She didn't stop to pray, having prayed without ceasing since the day began, so caught was her eye in beauty each minute. On that winter day when grey was king at my cottage and this colorful catalogue spilled out of my mail, I nearly ordered a pound of poppy seeds. And they don't even grow in my New York climate!

Another day, more modest in its threat to our movement, *Jackson and Perkins* "Home Gardening Excellence Since 1872" showed up in the mail. *Jackson and Perkins* have made their name most recently by selling a cheap variety of hardy fence roses, the color of which is certainly not grey but has that repeatable, interchangeable quality that is threatening to become one position above grey. Since everyone in nearly every community has bought these fast-growing pink roses, the world is beginning to format to a Jackson and Perkins color code. We need to resist these conformities when and as we can. First it was marigolds and now this!

Jackson and Perkins in this new edition was moving on, beyond the roses. Their cover was cottage garden. The house behind the cottage had its door seductively open to show an easel and a few paints. People in these houses don't do dishes or have dustballs under their couches. They spend their days painting and gardening. If we buy items from these catalogues, perhaps we may enjoy the same leisure.

J and P (1-800-292-GROW) wants to sell me a hammock from that now famous Pauley's Island, wicker, infantile garden sculptures, planters that are much more respectable and expensive than the recyclables I now use, botanical prints, English picnic baskets, and some delightful astilbes. Clearly they are trying to move up a notch in social class. The astilbes come in both a pink and a white feathery style that demonstrate the genuine concern J and P has for color and its variations. I not only should, but did, order them and they were worth the $6.95 per. They have a respect for the variety of pinks that our movement need not fear paying for.

Now that we have established the importance of fantasy and the importance of color to our resistance movement against the bland, the grey, and the conforming, we are ready for *Gardener's Supply* which offers innovative gardening solutions. These people imply by their slogan that there are problems in gardening, and there are. We need the pragmatist to round out our little sermon. *Gardener's Supply* sells a variety of hoses, planters, fertilizers, kneelers, edgers, teepees, and stakes, composters—even one described as the Cadillac of composters, tools to stir up composters, shredders, etc. These tools give our movement the kind of infrastructure it needs if it is to be taken seriously. By calling 802-863-1700 or writing to them in Burlington, Vermont 05401,

128 Intervale Road, you can outfit yourself for the long haul of making fantasy and color survive. That they provide free environmental gardening bulletins shows that they not only have products that sustain us, but that they are also aware of sustainability as a public value. Of course you can always stir your homemade compost pile with a stick and sustain yourself that way too.

Now it is summer and I'm glad for the astilbes that I ordered instead of all those poppies. I really like my compost stirrer. I enjoyed these items when I ordered them and I am enjoying them now. Spring is clearly the foreplay to summer's sex. Then we hoped, now we realize hope.

By fall we will be remembering these realized hopes and stocking our arsenal against the inevitable return of the grey. Photographs are a good weapon. That's one of the things the seed catalogues return to tell us in the spring. They snap flax and poppies and California women at their peak. They wait till the dishes are done and the easel properly set up to click their camera on the finest day August provides. They put on their boots on days when there is no mud and line them up on fancy doormats, there-by selling us tools to sustain our movement.

I have two photos on my desk. They are not orgasmic memories but rather arrows in the quiver of my resistance. One is just a bunch of zinnias, arranged on the porch of a beach house a friend loaned me one year. The zinnias are set between the two rocking chairs on which we sat to view the bay. I can look over when I am writing and rock a little despite the fact that the zinnias only lasted three good days.

The other photo is of my two sons in shirtless overalls, running down a Vermont hill late in August and early in their life. They are holding hands. Yes, these are the same two boys who touch each other every day but not always in affectionate ways. They are running towards the garden with the green beans we ate that night for supper. Over the hill a bit are the Green Mountains, shouting resistance, covered with wildflowers sufficient for a lifetime of color and fantasy. The picture doesn't show all this. It just reminds me that it is there, and that at least one summer I saw it. Now these photos sustain me against the return of the grey.

Without the seed catalogues, far too many pictures would be lost.

Teaching My Daughter To Mulch

The Return Of The Push Mower

I t's hard to say just how the anti-lawn movement got started. Or why it was that the push mower came back. People say it was on Father's Day late in the last century. Someone published a piece in the paper of record suggesting that the White House Lawn be abolished. The environmentalists had long been screaming about fertilizers and how they wash off the lawn into the wells and oceans, fouling up one balance after another. The fitness types gave up their power lawn mowers for aerobic purposes easily a decade earlier; this loss of the capacity to maintain had already made the lawn smaller. One man, the father of the man who managed to suggest abolishing the white house lawn, actually mowed his initials in the weeds in front of his house because his neighbors complained so loudly about the mess he called his front yard.

When gas went to five dollars a gallon, lawn mowing took on a new cachet. Only the rich could afford big lawns. Pachysandra companies took over chemical fertilizer companies, and most people made a rough adjustment to the new realities of crabgrass. But not without a vintage form of suburban anguish.

Some people still wanted a little lawn. They could give up the chemicals in favor of a less vivid green but they couldn't give up green altogether. The gender politics of lawn mowing also played a part. Men were helping women with the dishes and diapers much more than women were helping men with the lawn. The Betty Friedan of the men's movement was never found but still, men's consciousness raising groups flowered nationwide. Women were put on notice: men were not going to waste all their leisure time mowing even little lawns.

The decision to buy stock in push mowers was a crucial one for the men's movement. They watched women try to start power mowers and knew that there would be no justice without a more appropriate technology. Women, oddly, agreed.

Most people credit Joe and Amy Ferguson with the real return of the push mower. Their pioneering family laid the ground work for all the others; the story, now embellished, is this:

Amy had agreed with Joe about the justice of sharing lawn mowing. No matter how much fun her friends made of her for not being feminine enough, by God, she meant to mow the lawn. But every time she went outside to mow, she was frustrated by the power mower. She tried to start it, her youngest son tried to start it, and her oldest son tried to start it. Like most of the men who had ever been in her life, these two offspring couldn't bear the sight of her being mechanical. Thus they made man-sounding noises and yanked on the lawn mower chain. Amy yanked on it with equal effort and no noises. Nothing happened. Joe came out and yanked on it with both boys gazing fondly at his muscles, listening eagerly for his noises. Still nothing happened. When he became hysterical and mumbled spark plugs over and over—realizing that there was no freedom if he had to still master the machine—Amy made her decision. She would get a lawn mower that she could push. She would not bother Joe any more. He had learned detergents, she would learn mowing.

She went to three hardware stores in search of a push mower. Three times she was turned down. First by someone who, between chews, indicated that there wasn't much *call* for them anymore. The second guy actually laughed at her. The third guy looked at her ring finger and just shook his head. She had to endure disparagement of Joe. At the fourth store the man thought he had one left somewhere and, sure enough, he produced it, in a box, which she knew meant trouble.

The box meant that it wasn't standing up, and if it wasn't standing up, that meant she would have to bother poor old Joe with it. The whole point of this expedition was to keep him out of it. She didn't want to take a whole course in screw drivers and bolts, so she told the salesman she'd take it if he'd find somebody to put it together. He said, "Five dollars more," she said, "Sold!" he said, "Don't you want to see it first?" and she said, "Of course not." She didn't need to fondle it, just use it.

She did tell Joe that had she been more of a person, while those hardware store men were cautiously discussing the assembly with each other and doing a little bit of it at the same time, she would have gotten out her nail file, sat on an air conditioner box and done her nails. Just for the effect. Each man had assured the other that he didn't know too much about these old machines *but* they got it together. Fifteen minutes later, Joe's wife was home and mowing. No muss, no fuss. No gas, no spark plugs. No husbands to program. Her glee was girlish and unbounded.

Both of her boys (but not her daughter) insisted on a turn behind the mower. She refused their request. Blowing hard, getting her heart rate way above its Wednesday morning aerobic level, she mowed the lawn. It was sheer bliss. Clack, clack, clatter, clatter. Except for having to move the curious kids vigorously out of the way every now and then, there were no obstacles. What she enjoyed most was the sound of the engine. There was no sound to the engine. None at all. Joe wasn't bothered by either the kids or the noise. He was peacefully watching the ball game, having finished folding the laundry. Amy couldn't have been more pleased.

Until their neighbor appeared. He came over and demanded to know what she was doing. Clearly he was concerned that Joe might be embarrassed by what his wife was doing right on the front lawn. The neighbor was so offended for Joe that he not only asked the question, he came over the next day and redid the area she had mowed with his riding power mower. Yes, he did. When Joe came home the next afternoon, sure enough, there he was riding over their mowed lawn. Joe was astonished. Imagine a guy like that being so hung up on his own masculinity that he couldn't let his wife enjoy a little power, a little exercise, a little relaxation.

It was the radical pioneering of Joe and Amy Ferguson, against all obstacles, in the early part of the 1990s, that led to the tradition of buying push mowers for Fathers on Fathers Day. Or so say the anti-pachysandra people.

Teaching My Daughter To Mulch

Teaching My Daughter To Mulch

Summer Gardens

both love and hate to travel in the summer. So sums up the gypsy theory of life. Can't stay, can't go. To leave one's own garden in its hyperactive time is painful. The only balm is the ability to see another's garden. I go to Star Island now regularly. There I imagine that Celia Thaxter's famous garden is mine. The fantasy comforts me till I get home.

This summer borrowing all began when I was called to be chaplain for a week at Star Island, an island six miles off the coast of Portsmouth, New Hampshire. I couldn't have picked a worse sermon topic for my first six-day series at Family Camp if I had tried. "Hope in Hard Times" it was called. The first day I stood at the pulpit in the Gosport Chapel and stared out at the rock's intimacy with the ocean, all around. I remember thinking, "What hard times? Are there hard times somewhere? Is that possible?"

By boat, Star is a twelve dollar and one hour trip. The waves the Steamship Company calls moderate, most travelers experience as choppy. A good swell develops right out of the harbor, and that is the last time most people experience a hard time for their stay.

I was joining a United Church of Christ Family Camp. Others go for science camps, nature camps, or no theme camps, and they usually stay for one week each. The cost of the camp is about $250 per week and includes all meals, lodging, and program. Children come for half that and have organized activities most of the day.

I had come as volunteer staff and was much too selfish about the rest of my time on the island to redo my "Hope in Hard Times" series. Daily I asked the worshippers' forgiveness. Forgive me for allowing the mainland to intrude so fiercely on the island. We are here, I argued, to "retrue" ourselves—as one of the painters who came here long ago said. Retrueing must mean at least making the connections to the beauty here and the hard times on the mainland. The argument either worked or it didn't. I rather forgot about my performance and cared about mica and majesty instead. Mica is the rock that the island is made of; the children are given hammers and they go off to chip away at it. The adults are given the majesty of the surrounding sea; we chip away at that as well.

The United Church of Christ and the Unitarian Universalists own Star Island and use it for "religious and educational purposes." College students, called Pelicans, retrieve your bags right at the boat, and you walk to the grand old hotel up the hill, bowing as you greet her and she invites you to take one of the rocking chairs on the porch. I chipped away at the majesty from one of those chairs most of the week.

Fifty-four feet above the high water mark, the hotel is white clapboard and makes you want to put on a long dress for dinner. The island, first mapped by Captain John Smith in 1614, is only forty-two acres but seems as large as all outdoors. Horizons of the Atlantic on one side and a bright New Hampshire and Massachusetts coastline on the other, turn the trick of creating space out of succinctness.

At our Mini Chatauqua, one of over a dozen held each summer, week by week, the theme was Family Values. I came almost to believe in them again in the silent procession up the rocky path to the meetinghouse in the dark for the candlelight service that ends the day. The wrought iron hooks waited all day for the processional of light; once the lanterns were hung, and the music begun, electrified thoughts from the mainland met their nemesis.

So fond did I become of my forgetfulness from shore that I even forgot self-improvement. There were many events in which I did not even participate. The daily polar bear swims in an ocean that did not rise above sixty-five degrees were replaced by a cup of tea. I preferred the rather loud bell in the buoy to the sound of my teeth chattering. I wanted to focus all my attention on creation, not recreation. The bridge games and the tennis tournaments—on a truly awful court—part of Star's non-resort appeal, or the wildflower walks, and the open sings sounded too much like appointments, starting as they did, at specified times. I coveted the island clocklessness too much to do what I might otherwise have enjoyed.

I took full advantage of the excellent daily childcare provided by two long-term staff people who, in their shore life, educate Boston's children. My three cherubs spent their days mica mining on the rocks, exploring pirate caves, and hearing scary stories of times of yore. (It seems, in fact, that Molly, a first white settler, hid in a cave from genuine pirates and smothered her newborn to death while protecting her.) They reported these tales to me at the three excellent meals per day that we shared—and then took off. Forgive me also if I describe these brief visits, replete with excited narrative, as my ideal of childcare.

Star is one of nine islands in a group known as the Isles of Shoals. Shoal is an old English word for school of fish. Historian Fred McGill, a retired English professor who first visited Star in 1922 and has been back yearly ever since for the entire season, tells of what Star does to him. "It roots me. Funny isn't it, how all this tide could make you feel stable?"

Pelicans, college-age staffers, don't just bear the bags up the hill. They put on a superb talent show—hired as they are by needing to bring one talent or skill as well as a need for a summer job—and only choose one day a week to do cross-dressing in the dining room. Their sense of humor needs to be large: the guests are dependent on them to lug morning pitchers of wash water for their rooms. They must really appreciate faucets when they return to school.

If there is a difficulty at Star, it is water. Two showers a week are all the guests are permitted. In the morning, the Pelicans bring hot cistern water to the rooms in plastic buckets. So much of what is old-fashioned is pleasant; this feature is not, but is forgotten very soon, especially after everyone else's hair in the dining room starts looking a lot like yours.

The poison ivy is a seriously unmajestic aspect of the creation as are the seagulls. Much of the island is a biological tangle of briar and wild cherry, witch grass, and sumac, evidence of how much people have left it alone and God has allowed nature to carry on.

To keep the seagull population down, phony eggs have been placed around the island. These eggs trick the gulls into thinking they are having babies. More than just the Audubon Society cares what happens to birds on the island. There are times when the population of seagulls has seriously interfered with the mica mining of the children and the morning walks of the adults. Not wanting to upset the balance of nature in the place, or to let the seagulls prohibit human use of the island, many methods of population control have been used on the island. The phony egg method has worked, so far.

Star is the wilder of the islands in the Isles of Shoals. For horticulture you have to boat from Star to Appledore, a short trip across the harbor. There the famous Celia Thaxter garden exists. She is surely the most famous of the Shoals residents. Thaxter was a gifted writer, passionate romantic, and uncommon gardener. When it came time to restore her garden, former Islanders came from throughout New England, returning sprigs and seeds, bulbs and ideas, all of which their parents and grandmothers had borrowed from Appledore. The garden now is completely its old self. Sort of.

The hops vine on both Star and Appledore, as well as the tawny daylily, are Thaxter signatures. Despite more than seventy years of neglect, John Kingsbury, founding director of the Shoals Marine Laboratory on Appledore, was able to reconstruct the small garden completely in the last few decades. He even used Celia's old method of planting slips in eggshells and then burying them in the ground. There are people all over New England who have day-tripped to Appledore to leave old fashioned plants or to pick them up. In their purses they carry the eggshells.

Thaxter grew up on the Isles of Shoals, first on White Island, where as a lonely child, she grew marigolds, later on Appledore, where her family operated a resort hotel. At sixteen she wed her tutor, Levi Thaxter, a dreamer eleven years her senior. The marriage was difficult from the start and filled with lengthy separations. Celia filled her days with writing and gardening.

In her newly popular book, she says, "Mine is just a little old-fashioned garden where the flowers come together to praise the Lord." (1988) When she thought of praise, color, not layout, was her primary concern. The contrast of her bright colors with the island's varying bleached shades is truly spectacular.

Attracted in the last century to her place by her unassuming charm, such luminaries as Impressionist Childe Hassam, poet James Russell Lowell, and authors William Dean Howells, and Harriet Beecher Stowe made annual pilgrimages. When she died in 1894, her family maintained the garden for a few years but eventually left the island. In 1914 a fire destroyed her hotel complex and her cottage, then the garden disappeared. Now the fifty by fifteen foot garden looks as it did in the beginning. Searching antique catalogs for the plant names and then acquiring the roots from specialized nurseries, the Marine Laboratory was able to put things back together. The garden is open to the public only by permission from June to September by calling the Marine Lab at the Isles of Shoals, 607-255-3717.

Whenever, as a gypsy, you need to borrow another's garden for a while, here on Appledore there is one waiting for you. It is a wild place, mostly because of the hovering of the gulls. But Celia packed it with color. She tried to stabilize the wild island and did so for a few brief years at the hotel. But the wild won. The hotel burned down in an amazing blaze in the twenties and no one dared rebuild it. The garden's disrepair has now been changed but people now must see it surrounded by *nature* as opposed to *civilization*, whatever that distinction means.

The spiritual experience of Star is equally wild, equally unusual. Nathaniel Hawthorne knew it as that "stern and awful place." (Thaxter, 1988) More than one family vacation has been interrupted by the sternness of the place. At Family Camp this year, on his birthday, seven year old Joshua told some of the story of his birth. His mother delivered him seven years ago on the last day of family camp, after a quick Coast Guard ride home. Jordan, another camper was equally lucky but not immediately. When he got hit in the head with a baseball bat, on a morning when the whole camp was fogged in, the Coast Guard was finally able to get him to a mainland hospital that afternoon. He survives now with medication for his seizures. People call that the longest day on Star Island. Classes and chapel were canceled while people waited for the Coast Guard boat, or the fog to lift.

There are hard times, even on Star. Very few gardens grow simply. Most are as complex as growth or birth itself. Just like the education for religion that is supposed to be going on. And the chaplains who come in from time to time, to address the wrong subject, in their spare time.

Even, and especially, the gypsy gardener has to have hope. Hope for the delicate is hard to sustain when we don't see the long-term rewards for our efforts. Seeing Celia Thaxter's garden live and die and be reborn gave me hope for the delicate.

That hope had been particularly beaten down by one experience I had in my New York garden. There in the south garden, the weeds all went to military school and the flowers all went to finishing school. Peonies, sweet peas, and poppies are not strong enough to stand up to that green thing with the blue flowers only in the morning. It had taken over every year and smashed the lighter flowers to smithereens.

A smart gardener would have called the south garden the "green-thing-with-blue-flowers-only-in-the-morning garden" and left it at that. I ordered sweet pea seed.

My husband thinks it is my excessive openness to weeds, my lack of early pulling, that causes this war between fragility and toughness to happen in more than just the south garden. Like the mentally ill man who painted our house, sort of, that summer. He made the toughness of gardening seem mild.

I think it's a decision not to let the weeds go into the harsh world alone and uncomforted. It is also a choice to show all the sides of God and garden. It is actually a hope for the delicate.

One choice, under these circumstances, is to plant only nasturtiums. They wave the same in the breeze as sweet peas and have an equal lightness. They might have more of a chance against the green thing, and they don't require the soil to be fussed with so before planting. If anything, they like a poverty stricken soil, insufficient moisture, and weird trace elements. Sweet peas are just the opposite. Only a well laden, richly fed table for them. If their wine glass is empty, even between courses, they die.

But the nasturtiums are too easy. When they survive, there is no comfort in it. Like a child born for school and raised in a home where books are everywhere, their victories come too easily. As a gardener, I prefer the tougher cases—if for no other reason than to magnify the miracle of growing, to see it on its true terms. Like the man who sort of painted the house, the delicate species enjoy a larger success. You have to measure their progress from the point at which they started, not from the point at which the average person or plant starts.

My patron saint in these matters is Celia Thaxter. She gardened in one of the most hostile environments imaginable. If Celia can grow poppies and sweet peas on what Hawthorne called the island's "Bare-blown rock," (Thaxter 1988) then I can grow them in the south garden.

There is no point in wearing a hat on Appledore. It will blow off. Sun dresses are equally frivolous. A sturdy sweat shirt is what you'll need. And yet, Celia, eight miles out to sea off the coast of New Hampshire, grew poppies. Shirley poppies to be exact. She started all her seedlings in egg shells. More fragile you cannot get.

When she heard that toads were good at prohibiting certain pests, she ordered a breed from France! This purchase, before the days of UPS, which might itself have trouble getting the toads to Appledore, is an act of courage on behalf of the garden. Just the logistics of it all bother me.

But they did not bother Celia. Her favorite plant was the sweet pea. Blue, rose, pink, and white. The idea of those sweet peas battling the ocean wind is enough to inspire any gardener. Hollyhocks you can understand, although even these, another Thaxter signature, don't like to be blown about once they get tall.

The delicate need courage more than the strong. The strong have their strength. The delicate have miracles behind them. When James Russell Lowell commented that here, on Appledore, "you are so near to the great heart of God that you can almost hear it beat," (Thaxter, 1988) I wonder what he meant. Was he referring to the great and mighty wind, the all-mighty, all-powerful, all-knowing, the one we call the everything God—and some of us call the totalitarian—or might he have been referring to the strength in the tides? Or the severity of the rock? Or, might he have been referring to delicate beauty, colored petals that survive the storms, that lift up after being beaten down? Might he have seen clear through to the heart of God, that place where the weak, miraculously, are protected?

He could also be talking about the multiple personalities of the divine. Hollyhocks that bend with the wind and those that topple, Shirley poppies and that green thing that only blooms in the morning. Men who were born to paint and men who can't attach to paintbrushes. Even nasturtiums and their ability to get by on almost nothing or sweet peas and their insatiability. Both strength and weakness, competence and incompetence, delicate and sturdy? All this and more deep in the heartbeat of God?

It's hard to say. We can never really know which God another sees. Celia thought you could get toads to Appledore and did; my painter thought he couldn't paint and didn't.

Of course Celia kept her flowers short. To do otherwise was to tempt both wind and fate beyond the risky limit she already challenged. She also kept her garden small, fifty feet by ten feet, a riot of delicate color but concise, to the point, not roaming beyond the safety of a hill above and a hill below. The-tall-green-thing-with-the-blue-flowers-only-in-the-morning would not make it here. It would be blown over by the first Nor'easter. Not to mention that its proportion of green and growth to blue and needly was too small. You have to bloom vigorously to stay in the delicate garden.

If there is to be hope for the delicate, you probably also need a particular kind of gardener. Almost God-like, the type that is off rounding up lost sheep. Listen to Celia's self-description: "I garden to love up. To nourish. To cherish things into health and vigor." (1988) This from a woman who spent sleepless nights over the matter of slugs. It is dangerous to be delicate. You need protection. You need a gardener who doesn't mind the softer verbs of nourish and cherish, those words that have the same strong sound of a heartbeat, the same sound of sweet peas whispering in a soft breeze. The delicate have no hope if all the gardener can do is hoe and dig, rake and stake. But the delicate have hope, even in my south garden, if they intend to whisper the word miracle and to do that to the breeze.

All these lessons I would not have known had I not found the pain of being away from my own garden in the summer. The gypsy gets things that those who stay at home can never imagine.

Teaching My Daughter To Mulch

Teaching My Daughter To Mulch

Pulling Up

oving a garden is a lot easier than most people think. The reason is that gardening is about the garden—and it is the gardener who moves, not the soil. Just last night my husband wanted to know if I wanted to bother planting the soup's fish heads in next year's tomato spot. Did I want to bother, since we are moving in a matter of weeks? Of course I wanted to bother. Somebody will till this soil if not me. I may be moving my garden, but I am not moving *the* garden. Garden is means, not end; process, not product; spiritual not physical. Spiritual processes are light as a feather. You just pick them up and bring them with you.

My daughter accuses me of only wanting to move to the new house on West Street in Amherst because of the garden. (She prefers the place on Bay Road with the horse barn.) She is absolutely right. I took one look at the ancient English Cottage garden west of the house and said I'd take the place. I was not swayed in this original judgment by the appearance of asbestos on the burner or red velvet wallpaper in the living room. That garden would save me years. For the first time in years I wouldn't have to build one from scratch. I could build on someone else's beginning.

I say this with respect for that part of gardens which is backbreaking work, which is end, product, and physical. You can do something about each of these matters if you have the other skills. The other skills are the courage and the heart to garden. They are spiritual skills, maybe even lusts. They carry the weight.

I know about this ease with which gardens move because I have moved so many. Tucson moved to Pennsylvania. And Tucson was a city garden with desert earth. It was a tough garden, but it still produced strawberries—the second year. Pennsylvania was a comparatively easy garden. It was built on an ancient ruin. The weeds grew as well as the plants. Southeastern Pennsylvania moved to Philadelphia which moved to New Haven which moved to Amherst which moved to Chicago which moved to the eastern end of Long Island which is now moving back to Amherst. I was in Chicago twice also but one time as a student and then I didn't think I needed to garden. Persephone and I like to return.

I have never stayed long enough for the asparagus to come up. Still, in all the places, except Tucson, Philadelphia, and Chicago—where space was at a premium—I planted asparagus. The only thing I regret is the expense. It comforts me to know that someone else has what might have been considered *my* asparagus.

I created a mythological plant, named Ruby Begonia, who is a whore. She follows me everywhere and makes her living on the street. Otherwise when a garden is kissed goodbye, it is gone. I expect no followers and don't usually even take cuttings or bulbs. That modest form of theft I reserve for other people's gardens. After all, I have given other people a lot of asparagus, why shouldn't I reap a bulb or two?

Once you have the courage and the heart to garden, moving is easy. Understanding that gardening is a low cost form of personal entertainment allows moving to be light. Moving doesn't mean you stop going to the movies; therefore it shouldn't mean that you stop gardening. Lightness always moves easy.

The gypsy in me appreciates at least three things about gardens: their lightness, the importance of the natural redistribution of things (what some see as stealing), and the entertainment.

First the lightness. We usually buy our houses for the gardens rather than the houses. (Which may be one reason we have been so miserable in these 900 square feet for six years.) The gardening impulse bought this house on the eastern end of Long Island. What was here was land and forest. We had to clear the half acre of forest before we could even start the garden. The congregation of the church here had the same opposite-of-effortless feeling—and that's another reason to leave them and try another. I haven't told the kids that yet. They'll find out soon enough that some people don't want to bloom, process or no process.

The way to clear a half acre of forest is to put up a sign in your front yard that says "free wood." The men who are married to the women who clip coupons show up with chain saws. Granted, they leave unsightly stumps, but vine hides them well. Plus, in a flat land, a little elevation helps.

Once the forest is cleared, especially if it is this close to the sea, the sand needs to be built up. Mild winters make it possible to do this in almost two years—granting, of course, that no one has raked leaves on the property for a decade. After that, the only real cost is the lime. The lightness of gardening is not only spiritual; it is also directly proportional to how many other people are doing the heavy work. The wonderful part about this community was the way people helped each other, bloom or no bloom. I always felt they just didn't have enough light.

Similar principles apply to the redistribution of garden wealth. If you want to own your asparagus, then you will feel too attached to it. If you want to own your labor, it will become too heavy. The heaviness will come from the attachment. Giving it away as you grow it—whether the gift be wood or asparagus or your labor when next door wants to clear—keeps the heaviness of ownership from invading the entertainment of gardening. And the entertainment will never be as expensive as the movies.

Pulling up a garden is easy once we understand what gardens are. They are light, inexpensive forms of entertainment. They don't move; we move.

Our efforts have resulted in soil worth planting in. Our soil granted thirteen kinds of Italian lettuce last year as well as over one hundred red raspberry bushes in maturity. (The raspberry bushes came courtesy of two families in the congregation who did know how to grow.) The asparagus is still, after all this time, discontented with its lot. It will come. The strawberries look good but they don't produce enough. I think lime may have been overdone in their neighborhood. The Chinese green beans loved it in that location. (Location, location, location say the real estate people.) Sweet peas never grew here either, but I have a feeling that they will this year. Not just born of my own optimism, this is an educated feeling. I know they are heavy eaters, but really! I have given them enough already. This year I have an entire rabbit hutch of rabbit waste. I think it will work.

The snow peas couldn't have done better. But basil hated its place in the rotation this year, and its failure particularly bothered me as my dear friend in Massachusetts reported growing three new kinds. And on and on, with that series of successes and failures, jealousies and victories, that making a garden implies. Lightness towards the failures helps; otherwise you can get really bogged down.

The front yard was an even better example of this repetition of fun and failure. Because there wasn't enough sun the first year, even after the forest was cleared in the back—due to the neighbors' not wanting to give away any free wood—we plowed up the front yard. It became easy to tell people which place was ours, "The only one on the street with the garden in front." The neighbor who was not going to like us anyway flipped out and called central zoning only to be told that you can do whatever you want with your front yard. He also called about the goats, the chickens, and the rabbits in the back yard and was told the same thing.

The front garden had its origin in conflict. When we put about a dozen bags of rather chunky cow manure into the plowed up front garden, he was apoplectic. "You have a lot of @@@##$$%%%% in your front yard." I renewed my prayer that when I retired I would have more to do than pick up each leaf as it dropped on my zoysia grass. It had not helped that the one time the dog got out she pooped on his zoysia grass. Of all the people in the neighborhood on whose property she might have pooped! The children developed an enemy out of it anyway, and every child needs one genuine enemy. He fit the bill perfectly.

In the front yard, because of the sun and the heavy manure, the garden took off the first year. I brought in the expensive peonies straight from the high-rent nursery in Litchfield, Connecticut. By the second year they were magnificent. We didn't have any other place to put the pear trees we had been given for an earlier Christmas, so we just stuck them in out there too. They are now so big they look kind of ridiculous. I am thinking of pulling them up and taking them to Massachusetts, although I have a terrible feeling that doing that well in this mild a winter will mean that they won't do so well where the winter is a more serious opponent to personal and agricultural warmth.

The mums I collected from several states gave good old burnt orange a real run for its money. And they came up every year. But the real runaway victory in the front garden has been the love affair between the cosmos and the morning glory. Three years now we haven't been able to plant a thing, so joyous have they been in their arrangement. Bloom, bloom, bloom. The glories climb the pear trees which makes for a bit of a hodge podge. But now that we have picked up every stake-like thing within five miles, you should see their ostentation. And I do try to keep them off the pear trees.

Obviously, the climate and the cows and the free-wood people kept the process light here. So did the stealing, which I prefer to see as redistribution. The moral basis is here: if I leave asparagus all over the country, why shouldn't I pick up what other people leave behind when I move?

People see our old green Volvo station wagon coming, and they add to their recycling piles. Recycling is one of the more sophisticated ways to redistribute the wealth. People know we can probably use some of what they have put out. The stakes have been a real delight to find. I even found some pretty wrought-iron ones that were actually meant for use in the garden. The rest are dead brooms and the like.

It all started with the leaves. The way we raised the forest in the back yard was by hauling everybody else's leaf bags. Our sign "free bagged leaves" didn't produce the way the free wood sign did. The children loved hauling leaves, proving Maria Montessori's point once and for all, that real work is more fun than real play. We probably hauled five hundred leaf bags the first year alone. And that's why our children may be leaf-pile jumpers when they grow up. It's their strongest skill.

The back yard suffers, some of our friends tell us, from our penchant for recycling. Two of our closest friends have actually said to us that we'd better do "something about it" if we want to sell the house before we move. And God knows, we want to sell the house before we move. We bought this 4br bath cape at the height of the Long Island real estate boom for $140,000. Then we put in $20,000 for skylights and other things you have to buy and can't rummage for. We bought it for the land which faces the oldest living white pine preserve in the Northeast, no doubt an environmental accident. (It's all swamp so you can't build on it.)

While our children were winning the leaf-jumping competition, our local economy has won prizes in the national recession competition. We couldn't sell this place for $110,000 if we wanted to. That's what we owe the bank. So sure, we'd like to sell it. Our friends, who are more suburban in their point of view, think the property won't sell until we cover over the compost pile, remove the goats, rabbits, and chickens, take out the huge tire the kids play on, etc. etc. I'd as soon kill my mother.

What they don't know is that the first ad I put in the local paper, "In-town organic farmette on one acre near forest preserve, for sale for a lot less than it should or did cost," drew dozens of inquiries. None of the people had any money but still there is a market for a place with this much already planted. Even in Riverhead which would like to think it is long past its organic roots but isn't.

From my point of view this property is nothing if not a steal. Or a redistribution of wealth. Either way, understanding that allows pulling up an appropriate lightness.

Plus, you should meet the people who came to look at the house. Five Ukrainian immigrants, one a medical doctor working as an orderly at the local hospital; a Baptist Evangelist and his wife who didn't think the basement was big enough for services; two group homes for retarded children; and at least a dozen single mothers with that many children each, it seemed. So far not one of them has been the slightest bit daunted by the size of the garden.

We did have one family of European background with two kids, who looked a lot like we do, show up. They were gone in a flash. They even had the money for the rent.

Before we pull up, somebody will show up who likes the garden and has enough money to pay what we owe the bank each month. One thousand dollars. Per month! Now that is what I call stealing. Heavy handed, not entertaining stealing. At least we have the garden and can take it with us. Lightly redistributing wealth is a good description of gardening.

That this garden has sneaked in between forest and house so easily will make it a particularly hard one to leave. But it belongs here and I don't anymore. It is almost out of respect for each other that we part.

Our place will someday sell to just the right person because it is too idiosyncratic to sell to the wrong person. Because gardening ranks very high on the list of cheap ways to have fun, only a fun-loving gardener is going to go for it. The recession can only heighten its value over time. Like walking, sex, and reading, gardening costs only the labor of appearing. Someone on the hunt for that kind of bargain will soon appear. (Or we'll rent it to a half dozen Ukrainian immigrants.)

The third leg of the lightness is the entertainment. If the first is the way spiritual resources create partnerships in which they outweigh physical difficulties and the second is socialist, the redistribution of wealth, then the third is surely the low cost form of entertainment.

Gardening differs slightly from the simpler forms of cheap fun. You can find lots of ways to spend money on the garden. In January and February the seductions abound. I did fantasy seed buying the other night and managed to total a $200 seed and nursery order. It was the new roses and the astilbes that did it, although that many campanula are bound to add up. I won't send all these orders, but it was fun to let my credit card enjoy itself for the evening. Even if we are moving, I still like to spend my winter evenings this way.

When we left Arizona, I did winter buying after figuring out how to grow flowers in the downtown desert there. (Recycle water.) I still ordered seeds the winter we moved back to the farm in Pennsylvania and the winter we moved to Chicago. In both places, the first because we had no money and the second because we had no land, the gardening was really about the same as it has been here—more mental than physical. More a low cost form of personal entertainment than a thing that actually had to happen. Even though we have produced an actual garden here, the pleasure has been mostly spiritual.

The spiritual fun of it consists in the practical challenge: how to keep the entertainment low cost and personal. I have discovered at least two practical ways to keep the costs down and the fun up in the garden. One is the idea of a bulb bash.

Apparently this idea has been circulated as widely as its barn raising predecessor. I, who previously thought she had considered every way to survive without money, having bartered a funeral for a will from a lawyer, baptisms for tulip bulbs, and weddings for sauerkraut made the right way, community organizing for red raspberries, etc., was astonished to be informed of the bulb bash. Simply, you have a party in which everyone brings and plants a bulb or perennial. Your garden grows because your friends have extra of this or that. You spend the time normally used for cocktails in directing friends to previously dug, composted manured holes. They plant their offerings. From then on your tulips remind you of Susan, the phlox of Norman, the peach tree of Gene. Personalized, without those awful delivery charges at the end of nursery orders, planted—how much more thrifty can you get? And, starting the cocktail hour later is no sin.

Early spring or late fall parties can be had in the same year. The only warning is to not return peaches to Gene (he doesn't need them) or tell Susan you don't like that color there. Feelings are fragile. When your friends have their bulb bash, you need to bring something new. You might eventually need one of those books that old-fashioned hostesses used to have—broccoli divan when the Chesterfields were here in 1972—just to make sure you don't serve it if they come again.

Another way to keep the gardening costs down and the diversity high is to steal perennials. There is no point in obfuscation. During most of the growing season here, I always wear the pants with the big pockets for my walks. Seed catching has made my wildflower patch a real dream. I find the strongest flowers in the field and steal their seeds. They don't mind. They are glad to be useful, to be fruitful, and to multiply.

I have been caught on country roadsides with a shovel, digging up daylilies that had a good bright or raspberries that were overgrown. The people who catch me usually pull out their own shovel or consent to let mine do the work for them. These roadside galas are too infrequently pruned. They need me to help them prepare for their next year's show. I would never touch a plant or even a seed with a house close by. I would never take a whole plant, only its excess. I always mark the asparagus in the fall when they sprout their Christmas tree balls on their ferns. That way I can find them in the spring when they show up and not insult them by letting their hard work get big and hard and fall over, unnoticed and unappreciated. I can get two good meals of asparagus if I can take the time to make the hour-long drive it takes to gather all the rosebuds while I may. Obviously this is comfort for my failures in this area at home.

The abandoned doctors' offices in the middle of our ugly strip of malls provided me enough fresh roses for the entire month of June. I waited one full year before picking them and watched as they slowly went bad. I felt that I should get out my shovel and bring these orphans home, but that is close to the negative aspects of stealing. If, in one more year, no one takes over that office, I may have to move those roses to Massachusetts. They need fertilizer. They will die to the new owner on their own, should I not intervene.

They knocked over an old nursery, *The Bittersweet*, near this mall strip. They're building a huge grocery store on the spot. The nursery left behind hundreds of large planters, dozens of trellises, lots of dried up bulbs, and about 100 unsold Christmas trees from their last season. Our outdoor fireplace enjoyed some of their Christmas trees; I made half the bulbs grow; the trellises go great with the dead brooms; and I have given away dozens of the large planters. I picked the pumpkin off the vine that was just sitting there in the middle of the field before progress arrived. I am pretty sure I had comrades in this liberation of the useful from the debris; I could tell that somebody took some of the desiccated herbs which I had rejected. I'll bet they made them grow too.

One day I was driving past this spot and *The Bittersweet* was gone. It had disappeared. It was flat, brown dirt, with evidence of progress's tire marks everywhere in steamroller feet. I wished I had taken all the Christmas trees because they made a great bonfire. We burned our last at New Year's Eve on the stroke of midnight. I consoled myself with having done the best I could and immediately went to one of my forbidden raspberry patches to do some pruning for next year. It was the act of a mother who comes home from taking one of her children to the hospital with a broken leg and spends the rest of the night rocking the other one in the chair. Loss makes you tender.

I have spotted abandoned lupines on a road in Vermont, literally hundreds and hundreds of lupines, right next to a stream. I lust after them. But probably making the trip to Vermont would cost as much as ordering the few I would take. Plus my soil here doesn't have the wet feet in a sunny enough place for the lupines to grow. You know where I'll be late next summer.

Stealing does have limits. Gardening cheaply, however, does not. Pulling up roots would hurt too much if you thought you couldn't make another garden. Because you know you can, it's a bittersweet grief. One day you just wake up and realize that the Riverhead garden is gone. The New Year is on its way.

Some might even call the whole process progress. I prefer the notion of return. A return to the spiritual fun of the garden, only this time in a new soil.

Teaching My Daughter To Mulch

Teaching My Daughter To Mulch

Garden Infrastructure

e bought the new four-acre property in Amherst in November. The old stone walls were crumbling, the browned and deadened perennials announced unidentifiable life. Our excitement the first spring was uncontainable: everything that came up was a surprise. Lupine! Larkspur! Spearmint!

The second winter we got to work. Stones were our beginning. Rebuilding the stone walls when winter was withholding green proved to be a magnificent job. The cold managed the sweat of the effort. The outlines could be seen in a way that summer, fall, and spring prohibited. The canvas begged for large strokes.

The best move we made was to develop a new rock garden outside the kitchen window. There, in an old dog pen, though we couldn't see it while everything was growing, were broken fences, a nice slope, and a threshold to the rest of the property. It begged for planting. We refused the temptation to move the herb garden closer to the house. Good for tired feet at dinner time, bad to grow food in even ancient dog manure.

We gathered the rocks from the forest floor. Many of them were there, clearly forsaken by previous stone wall builders. Their odd shapes fit nicely into the slope of the hill. Rock gardens require more labor per square inch than other gardens but they return with an equal vigor. Moving stone is an ideal winter job and takes away what I call the itch of the pencil. In late winter, if I am not doing something with my garden, I am probably buying something with my credit card. Moving stone balanced my budget last year. And, because I opened a new space, all I had to do was steal perennials from myself in the early spring. The white nicotania adored the spot and so did the hollyhocks which climbed the white wall to the kitchen. I moved a couple of roses up near the warmth of the house and they did better there than the previous winter, forlorn next to the peonies. The real fun was the sunflowers, which planted themselves by the fallen-seed-from-the-bird feeder method. We are a very self-reliant household and we like the idea of our birds planting their own seed.

The winter joy of this garden is the stone. In the summer it clarifies and matches the flowers but in the winter it displays itself. Reginald Farrer, in *The Rock Garden* (1912), says that "stone is never disconnected; each block is always, as it were, a word in the sentence. A clump of unconnected rocks . . . is mere gibberish." An unidentified writer with the same point of view puts it like this, "There is no such thing as a half-built stone wall; it is either a wall or a stone pile." So it is with the kitchen rock garden, it connects us to the seasons. We also hauled rock from the Long Island Sound, where we used to live. It connects us to our old places. Now the children bring back rock for the garden from places we visit. Stone is always connecting, never disconnected. Such is the task of garden infrastructure: to keep things together.

Whatever you think your gypsy self is doing in the garden, she had better find her way to something eternal. All this change can get to you if you don't keep the fleeting aspect of time connected to the eternity of time. Rock gardens are your best bet. They become a new garden but use old stones. They are a way for old altars to meet and become new altars.

Everywhere we go, whether in the great Wall of China, the great castles of Europe, the pyramids of Egypt, or the biblical literature itself, which put the commandments, supposedly, on real stone, eternity is marked as the rock. Rock is the best metaphor we have of everlastingness, and gypsies, in particular, need to place rock around themselves.

As John Vivian put it so well in his introduction to *Building Stone Walls*, (1976), ". . . rock is as near a definition to forever as exists." He credits gravity with keeping rock sitting on top of itself; I credit larger spirits, the spirits within the stones that knew humanity needed a way to say permanent. Foundations may be slipping but the rocks are still there, almost begging for the reconnecting spirit of the gypsy gardener.

It is easy to make a rock garden on your property using old field stone. In New England particularly, there are thousands of old rock walls dotting the landscape. Many of these have already crumbled; some will go the way of farmland development into housing. Gathering fallen-away stone is not a recommendation to dismantle! Rather it is a slow, almost spiritual winter activity.

Finding and moving stone that has lost its connection to other stone is an act of beautification that can make an extraordinary difference in either a small or large way on a property.

Determining the spot for a rock garden on your land is easiest in February, after the snow has cleared and before the outline of the land has been changed by greening. The light of February's elongating days is particularly bright, in my view, and gives the gardener a welcome chance to evaluate land shapes. We all want something to do on behalf of the garden in the winter: taking a few days to site a rock garden is an excellent late winter activity. South facing is always best if you have it but other sites present other obstacles and opportunities. Both increase the beauty of the garden using the advice of great architects: they tell us to put the house in the place on the land where the land tells us to put it. Sometimes, the greater the challenge, the greater the product.

Often the most difficult corner on the property is the best place to use. Rock gardens love nooks and crannies, low spots, and high spots. They like to move themselves to fit the area. The plants we choose aren't as fussy as most in terms of soil. And rock gardens are equally open to shade or sun and points in between.

The February designer needs to remember that light will be much different in other seasons and not site for winter lighting alone.

Finally, siting should be based on imagining how the rocks will look in the non-green seasons as well as the green ones. One of the great pleasures of the rock garden is its year-round interest.

Thus its shape and its design are as important to the larger eye as the small eye, the distant and the close one.

The most beautiful spot around here is at Amethyst Brook in East Amherst. People have built a marvelous brookside series of cairns; a monument to what, I don't know. I keep hoping I can get some alpines, anonymously, in their vicinity. A rock garden built by no one anyone knows, used by the public, is a delightful idea of eternity to me.

Once you know how many stones you will need, it is time to begin your search. You may already have seen a crumbled stone wall in a field. Or you may have a rock pile already on the property. Or you may be in need of a back-road trip. Here you will find many stones falling onto state highways.

A more meditative way to proceed is to remember which places have been special to you in your life, both near and far. Where do you vacation? Where were you born? Where were you married? It could be time for a visit to these places to pick up rocks. Small rocks can be as interesting in a rock garden as large ones can. While shells often get messy in the garden, sometimes these beach finds have a place in a sentimentally oriented rock garden. Different types of stones can cohere in silly ways or interesting ways: keeping them separate enough so that they don't get busy but connecting enough so they show a pattern is the trick. A wave design for a path, for example, can incorporate many varieties.

"Gonna take a sentimental journey" is not a bad hum for moments like this. No one has to know you're singing, and the rock garden that results may or may not want to divulge its sources.

Hauling the stones is the hard part. In the old days, people built special equipment to haul the stones they wanted, today we have to depend on friends. Another way to get the rock you want is to have a rock-hauling party. Don't be afraid of large rock! You can get it without killing yourself but you have to have patience and take care. Lift only with your legs! A sprained back will add interest to the garden over time, but not in the first few days after the rock arrives.

To move and lift large rock, you need a crow bar and a friend. Or a stone boat and a roller; you ramp the stones to the site.

Obviously local stone is the best to use so hauling is kept to a minimum. On the other hand, I rarely leave a foreign country without one or two rocks in my suitcase. They make excellent souvenirs.

The goal of a rock garden is continuity between the rocks. The best designs happen when every major rock overlaps every other; the worst when rocks are dots in the middle of dirt. Rocks need to be placed and replaced. Be prepared for some give to avoid frost heaving. Corners and turns are the hardest spaces to fill; the rocks need to be sharp and they may take time to find. It may take years to find the right rocks. Shaping or dressing stone can be hard work and is not recommended for the amateur. On the other hand, there are still people around who are expert with the chisel and, if you have just the right stone, you may want to invest in their expertise. A smoother surface will enhance a wall's appeal.

Whether it is Helen and Scott Nearing hauling stone for decades to build their own "Good Life" house; or the Irish building altars or cairns in the fields; or the Christian use of rock as imagery for Lord, "the church's one foundation;" the one who said that if the disciples wouldn't speak, "even these stones would cry out", or the one whose temple they swore would be rebuilt in three days; or even the slang of being caught between a rock and a hard place or on a slippery slope; rocks *mean* things to people. Different things. Deep things. If you need a more devotional spot in your garden, rock is the way to go. You can make your own seat, and your own symbolism. You may want to review vows on its site or you may want to let its symbolism be open to whoever thinks whatever there. A site that is beyond the overturned bathtub and religious figure, still popular in a pious America and beautiful in its own way, is the direction you'll want to go if a spiritual garden is your destination.

Most rock garden plants like it cool and moist. The rock almost creates that kind of soil by its mulching factor. It is fairly easy to control the soil in a rock space so that you can be led by the plants and lighting you choose. Additive is easier to apply in a controlled space.

Some favorites for rock gardens include the primrose, which is clearly the gem because it requires so little space. The acaulis or English primrose bears a single flower on a short stem while the polyanthus has clusters of flowers on a longer stem. The garryarde is a short-stemmed polyanthus hybrid from Ireland with unusually dark foliage, while the juliana is a creeper that thrives in rocky crevices.

The creepers are my idea of survival specialists. They remind me of the poor as they find and make and keep a place to live. Like Jacob, they use rock as a pillow and dream great dreams of the holiness of their own crevice.

Echeveria, or hens and chicks, has several species native to Mexico. They are rosettes of leaves, often with red markings along the tips, which love sun and, as they are succulents, the soil must be allowed to dry before watering. They grow very close to the soil line but as they age they develop a stem. With time, the stem grows taller and taller with the rosette always clustering at the top. They are very eager to root and will grow quickly. Their value in a rock garden is the way they sneak through crevices to grow, always doing something unusual and unique to their spot.

For a more mixed garden, early tulips can be good. They have good carriage. You might also use arabis and golden alyssym, aubriettia, violas, polyanthus primroses, forget-me-nots, pansies, or English daisies. These are all spring bedding and would need companion planting for other seasons. Stay clear of big things, like caladiums, coxcomb, canna, or begonia rex. They overpower the rocks.

Finally, good plants can be borrowed from the forest floor. Never take something that is not well adapted to its own spot. Consider Eurasian wood, columbine, forget-me-not, mosotis, sylvatica, dutchmansbreeches, bloodroot, foam flower, any of the sedums, or wild blue phlox. The latter makes a sheet of clear blue that is very impressive.

Because rock garden plants are so congenial and grow so quickly if they like their location, they will almost always find their way from a neighbor's yard to yours. If you are only going to live in a place for a short while, and you know it, making horticultural friends is terribly important. They will remember you by what you took from their garden and made grow in yours. They will even tell the next *owner* the story. I have some magnificent red raspberries that still have a now-deceased friend's name on them. He gave me two sticks one fall and the patch is now a quarter of and acre and still marching toward the sun.

The uses of the rock garden as a site of beauty and meditation are many. As the great garden writer, Gertrude Jekyll, put it, "a rock terrace is always congenial to quiet thought." (1902) The process of building a quiet corner slowly and meditatively over time is its true meaning. Process over product, journey over destination, a work in progress—these are the long-term joys of building a rock garden. It never finishes nor does it have to. It will also last long after you are gone! But you will get enough connection, soon enough, to be secure in the eternity of having a quiet thought.

Teaching My Daughter To Mulch

Fall Crayons

n the field slated for development on Route 58, the competitions between the colors are in full swing. The wine berries have invited the antique bottles over for a deep blue competition. The mustards and golden rods have been bickering since breakfast about the relative merits of relative yellows. The purple asters have only the weary phlox left as rivals. The sumac has once again beaten the ivy in turning red, just as the pumpkins close in on orange.

The greens are out of it, their season being spring and this being very much not that. Spring is small and budding, gentle and pastel, incremental, rising, on its way up. This, fall, is big and baggy, harsh and bright, drooping when not dropping, on its way nowhere, just back home and arriving there sooner than anyone thought it would.

The colors quarrel, then settle their arguments. Some wisely know they are in their final season and savor their transformations while others, too young to really understand autumn, show off as if there were no tomorrow. They make fun of the dusty leaves in the way they recklessly yield themselves to every wind. The more sage protect themselves from buffeting, preferring stillness if possible.

The humans, immune from the wilds off Route 58 and their noisy pigmentations, are also deep in conversation. They too are talking about fall but the language is muted. Its colors range the hazy spectrum of loss. Maybe this is the last day for a bike ride at the proper temperature, which experts have declared to be seventy-five. Maybe the sheets will have to go in the dryer. I know it's going to be an early frost, I just know it. Gone are shirtsleeves. Gone is sunshine. The squirrels hide their harvest, the humans fill up their Ball jars, otherwise all of summer is lost.

One of the humans is sure to mention the oddity of mourning such a summer. They'll mention the rains, the length and duration of the record-breaking rains, the unbearable humidity. They will compete over mildew. Or they will complain about the heat. Neither the human nor the summer was all it hoped to be.

This conversation is also slated for development. It will develop into next summer, sure to be dry and cool, in a record-breaking sort of way. It will also pass on before its time.

Teaching My Daughter To Mulch

Teaching My Daughter To Mulch

Bibliography

Davis, Linda H. *Onward And Upward: A Biography of Katharine S. White*. New York: Harper & Row, 1987.

Farrer, Reginald. *My Rock Garden*. London: E. Arnold, 1907.

Francis, Robert. "Sing A Song Of A Juniper," In *Collected Poems, 1936-1976*. Amherst, MA: University of Massachusetts Press, 1976.

Fry, Christopher. *The Lady's Not For Burning*. New York: Dramatists Play Service, Inc., 1994.

Harlan, Jack. *Crops And Man*. Foundation For Modern Crop Science Series Vol. 1. Madison, Wisconsin: American Society of Agronomy, 1975.

Jekyll, Gertrude. *Wall And Water Gardens*. London: Country Life., 1902

Keeble, Midge. *Tottering In My Garden*. Ontario: Firefly Books, Ltd., 1989.

Merwin, W.S. *The Lost Upland*. New York: Alfred Knopf, Inc., 1992.

Sarton, May. *After the Stroke: A Journal*. New York: Norton. 1988.

Stein, Sara B. *My Weeds: A Gardener's Botany*. New York: Harper & Row, 1988.

Thaxter, Celia. *An Island Garden*. Boston: Houghton Mifflin, 1988.

Vivien, John. *Building Stone Walls*. Pownal, Vt. Storey Communications, Inc. 1979.

White, Katharine S. *Onward and Upward In The Garden*. New York: Farrar, Straus & Giroux, Inc. 1981.

About the Author

Donna Schaper is a writer and a minister. Days, she works as Area Minister or regional Bishop in the United Church of Christ, in spiritual charge of 120 churches in the Western Area of Massachusetts. Ordained in 1973, as one of the first women so to be, she worked as a parish pastor for twenty years, including a stint as Associate Chaplain at Yale University. She lives with her husband, Warren Goldstein, and her three children, Isaac, Katie, and Jacob in Amherst on a small farm.

She has just learned how to grow excellent spinach, her compost pile is steaming, and she has planted lupine in another three beds in her large garden. She mulches, mornings.